D1164813

RECREATE
MACHINE INNOVATIONS

CRABTREE
PUBLISHING COMPANY
WWW.CRABTREEBOOKS.COM

ANNA CLAYBOURNE

Author:
 Anna Claybourne
Editorial director:
 Kathy Middleton
Editors:
 Sarah Silver
 Elizabeth DiEmanuele
Proofreader:
 Wendy Scavuzzo
Interior design:
 Eoin Norton & Katherine Berti
Cover design:
 Katherine Berti
Photo research:
 Diana Morris
Print and production coordinator:
 Katherine Berti

Images:
All images by Eoin Norton for
Wayland except the following:
Alamy: North Wind Picture
 Archive: p. 18cl
Bel Pedrosa: p. 26t
Dreamstime
 Sergio Monti: p. 21b
 © Kaylene Kau. kayelenekau.com,
  Andrey Koturanov: p. 12cl
Fi Henshall: p. 22tr, 22cl
 Details from Wilhem Hondius,
  1644, Gdansk: p. 8tr, 8br
Getty Images
 Bettmann Archive: p. 16tr
iStockphoto
 Kaylene Kau: p. 28cl, 29br
 Wavebreakmedia: p. 5tl
NASA: Johnson Space Center: p. 4tr
NDSUL: p. 14tr
Polybius, The Histories, 1727
 edtion: p. 6cl

Shutterstock: front cover (airplane,
 barometer, pulley, gumball
 machine, stationery)
 Chameleon's Eye: p. 5br
 Christian Puscasu: p. 9br
 cowardlion: p. 4c
 halitomer: p. 6tr
 I Make Photo 17: 5bl
 Javier Garcia-Verdungo: p. 4bl
 Olesia Bilkei: p. 4br
 Photo and Vector: 21cl
 Radhu Razvan: p. 5tr
 Tae PY15MU: p. 15br
UISA: p. 16br
Wikimedia Commons
 Glane23: p. 27br
 PD: p. 10cl, 12tr
 Wellcome Images: p. 18tr
Every attempt has been made
to clear copyright. Should there
be any inadvertent omission
please apply to the publisher
for rectification.

Library and Archives Canada Cataloguing in Publication

Claybourne, Anna, author
 Recreate machine innovations / Anna Claybourne.

(Recreate scientific discoveries)
Includes index.
Issued in print and electronic formats.
ISBN 978-0-7787-5063-5 (hardcover).--
ISBN 978-0-7787-5069-7 (softcover).--
ISBN 978-1-4271-2155-4 (HTML)

 1. Machinery--Experiments--Juvenile literature. 2. Simple machines--
Experiments--Juvenile literature. I. Title.

TJ147.C53 2018   j621.8078   C2018-902459-3
                                           C2018-902460-7

Library of Congress Cataloging-in-Publication Data

Names: Claybourne, Anna, author.
Title: Recreate machine innovations / Anna Claybourne.
Description: New York, New York : Crabtree Publishing Company, 2018. |
 Series: Recreate scientific discoveries | Includes index.
Identifiers: LCCN 2018021348 (print) | LCCN 2018026368 (ebook) |
 ISBN 9781427121554 (Electronic) |
 ISBN 9780778750635 (hardcover) |
 ISBN 9780778750697 (paperback)
Subjects: LCSH: Machinery--Technical innovations--Juvenile literature.
Classification: LCC TJ147 (ebook) | LCC TJ147 .C55 2018 (print) |
 DDC 621.8--dc23
LC record available at https://lccn.loc.gov/2018021348

Crabtree Publishing Company

www.crabtreebooks.com   1-800-387-7650
Published in 2019 by Crabtree Publishing Company

First published in Great Britain in 2018 by Wayland
Copyright © Hodder and Stoughton, 2018

Published in Canada
Crabtree Publishing
616 Welland Ave.
St. Catharines, Ontario
L2M 5V6

Published in the United States
Crabtree Publishing
PMB 59051
350 Fifth Avenue, 59th Floor
New York, New York 10118

Note:
In preparation of this book, all due care has been exercised with regard to the
instructions, activities and techniques depicted. The publishers regret that they can
accept no liability for any loss or injury sustained. Always follow the manufacturers'
advice when using electric and battery-powered appliances.

The website addresses (URLs) included in this book were valid at the time of going
to press. It is possible that some addresses may have changed, or sites may have
changed or closed down since publication. While the author and publishers regret
any inconvenience this may cause to the readers, no responsibility for any such
changes can be accepted by either the author or the publishers.

Printed in the U.S.A./082018/CG20180601

CONTENTS

TAKE CARE!

These projects can be made with everyday objects, materials, and tools that you can find at home, or in a supermarket, hobby store, or DIY store. Some projects may involve working with things that are sharp or breakable, or need extra strength to operate. Make sure you have an adult on hand to supervise and to help with anything that could be dangerous. Always get permission before you try out any of the projects

HOW MACHINES WORK

Machines have made our lives easier since ancient times. Types of machines include waterwheels, bows and arrows, bicycles, dishwashers, and computers. We all use machines. Think about the machines you use every day. The television, the phone, and even a simple pair of scissors are all machines that are a part of life.

This robotic arm is on the International Space Station. It can pull supply space craft on board.

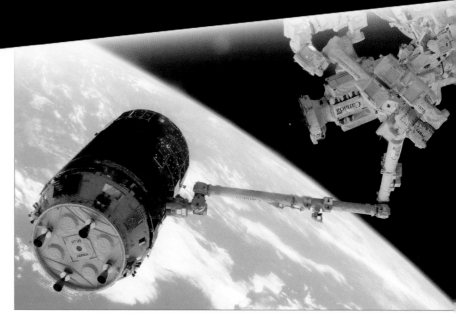

WHAT IS A MACHINE?

A machine is a device that helps us use forces to do a task. It doesn't have to be something with lots of moving parts. Many basic tools are **simple machines**. For example, a pair of scissors turns the squeezing force of your hand into pressure that cuts through material.

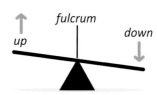

Of course, many machines have lots of moving parts, such as the **gears** inside a clock or the parts that make a helicopter, car, or robot.

HOW IT WORKS

Machines work by controlling and directing forces. One example is a **lever**. A lever is a straight bar with a pivot point or **fulcrum**, which rotates. It is an important part of many tools and larger machines.

up   fulcrum   down

When you press down on one end of this lever, the other end moves up. A seesaw is a simple lever.

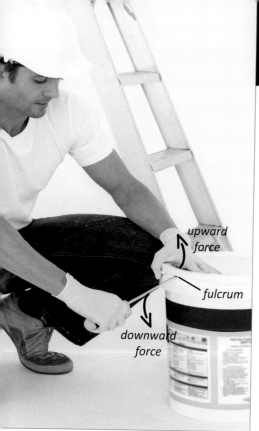

upward force

fulcrum

downward force

A solar-powered car in a special race for solar-powered vehicles and bicycles.

INVENTING MACHINES

Machines solve problems and achieve new things. The most important machines play a regular part in our lives. The wheel, printer, car engine, telephone, and computer are just a few of them! Today, people still make new machines all the time.

LEVER POWER

If the fulcrum is closer to one end, the short end will move a shorter distance than the long end. The shorter the distance, the more pushing power. That's what's happens when you use a spoon or screwdriver to take the lid off a jar.

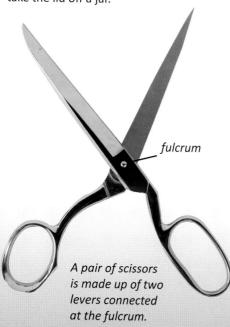

fulcrum

A pair of scissors is made up of two levers connected at the fulcrum.

MACHINE ART

Artists use machines to make art. They often use scissors, chisels, spray cans, and even computers. Machines can be art, too. Many modern artists make moving machine sculptures. There are drawing machines that draw their own pictures. There are machines that create light and sound. You can even make your own machines at home!

The Bucket Fountain, in Wellington, New Zealand, is a moving sculpture powered by water. It was designed by artists Burren and Keen.

THING FLINGER

Make a catapult inspired by Archimedes, one of the best makers ever.

A later illustration showing how one of Archimedes's catapults worked.

WHAT YOU NEED

- wooden craft sticks
- assorted elastic bands
- small wooden or plastic spoon
- a craft knife or scissors
- a small craft foam or cotton ball

ARCHIMEDES

(c. 287–212 B.C.E.)

Archimedes was an ancient Greek from Syracuse. This was a Greek settlement in Italy. Archimedes was a mathematician, scientist, and **engineer**. He also designed ships and invented machines. For example, he invented the **Archimedes screw** to pump water.

One day, the Romans attacked Syracuse. The city asked for his help to defend it from future attacks. Archimedes made many weapons. He made a claw for attacking enemy ships. He also made new catapult designs.

> Eureka! (I've got it!)
> **– reportedly shouted by Archimedes after he found the solution to a science problem**

1

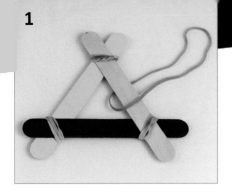

Step 1

Use three sticks to make a triangle. Wrap elastic bands around the ends. Before joining the last corner, link a strong elastic band onto the triangle.

2

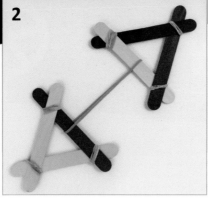

Step 2

Make another triangle the same way. Wrap the other end of the elastic band onto it.

3

Step 3

Roll the elastic bands at the corners so the ends poke out more.

4

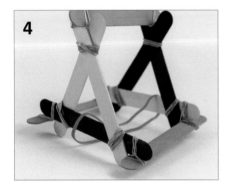

Step 4

Use more elastic bands to attach a stick between each of the two triangles at the corners. You should now have a frame made of sticks. Stand it up so the loose elastic band reaches across the bottom of the frame.

5

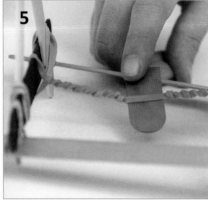

Step 5

Ask an adult to cut a short length of craft stick. Put it inside the loose elastic band, and twist it until the band is tightly twisted.

6

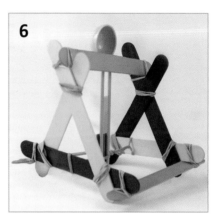

Step 6

Push the handle of the spoon into the twisted elastic band. You should push on top of the piece of stick, so the spon rests on the bar at the top of the frame.

7

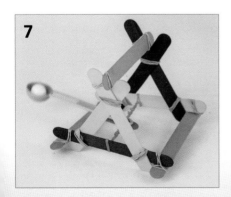

Step 7.

Holding the frame steady, pull the spoon down, then let it go. It should spring back up. Do it again, with a foam or cotton ball in the spoon. Ready, aim, fire!

STORING UP ENERGY

When you wind up the elastic band, the **energy** you use to twist the elastic gets stored in it. When you let go of the spoon, the stored energy gets released. This flings the spoon around in a circle. The bar at the top stops the spoon and the ball then keeps going. It flies through the air.

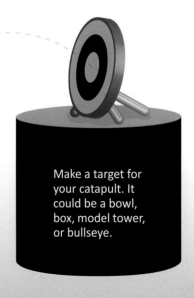

Make a target for your catapult. It could be a bowl, box, model tower, or bullseye.

CABLE DELIVERY

Build your own cable car to send messages, toys, or snacks to a location.

WHAT YOU NEED

- two plastic pulley wheels (from a hobby or hardware store or online)
- wooden skewers
- four wooden craft sticks
- a hole punch
- erasers or small corks
- strong yarn or string
- scissors or craft knife
- a small cardboard box
- a marker to decorate

Step 1

Ask an adult to cut a skewer into two 1.5-inch (4 cm) lengths using the scissors or craft knife. Push them through the center of each pulley wheel.

Instead of real pulley wheels, you can use the middle part of a medium or large Lego wheel, with the tire removed.

ADAM WYBE

(1584–1653)

Dutch engineer and inventor Adam Wybe designed all kinds of useful things. He made windmills, water wheels, bridges, and a fire-fighting water pump. His most famous creation was his aerial tramway, an early version of the **cable** car. He made it in 1644. Wybe's invention carried buckets of soil for building a city wall. It had a long loop of cable with more than 100 buckets attached. They circled around a set of **pulleys** on wooden towers.

An illustration of Adam Wybe's 1644 aerial tramway in Gdansk, Poland.

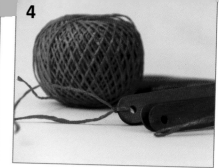

Step 2

With the help of an adult, use the hole punch to make holes in both ends of each craft stick. Put one stick on each side of the pulley wheels.

Step 3

Cut the erasers or corks if necessary. Push them onto the ends of the sticks to hold everything in place. Make sure the wheels can turn.

Step 4

Cut two 12-inch (30 cm) lengths of string. Use them to tie the other ends of the craft sticks together, leaving the long ends free.

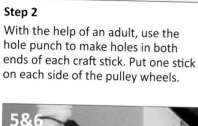

Step 5

With an adult to help, find two safe anchor points, one high and one low. You could use railings, coat hooks, window locks, or handles. If you can't find an anchor, ask an adult to put a nail or screw into a door frame.

Step 6

Tie your two pulleys to the anchor points. Then thread a long piece of string through both pulleys. Tie it tightly to make a loop.

Step 7

Use the cardboard box to make a cable car. Make triangular points on the side pieces. Punch holes in the tops of the triangles and tie a loop of string through them.

Step 8

Tie the cable car to the pulley cable, just above where you knotted it. You can now pull the cable at one end to make the cable car travel up and down.

SMOOTH MOVEMENT

A pulley wheel is a simple machine that allows a string or cable to move past a fixed point without resistance. It moves without rubbing or wearing away. It's a useful part of many machines, especially cable cars. Today, there are cable cars that carry people. They are all over the world.

POWERED FLIGHT

Copy the Wright brothers and make a plane.

WILBUR WRIGHT   ORVILLE WRIGHT

(1867–1912)   **(1871–1948)**

Orville and Wilbur Wright were American brothers. They made the first controlled flight of a machine that was heavier than air. They spent years making wings, **gliders**, and propellers. Then they made their famous flying machine, called the Wright Flyer. On December 17, 1903, the Wright Flyer had its first flight. It flew about 120 feet (36.5 m) with Orville onboard. Wilbur flew next!

> " The desire to fly is an idea handed down to us by our ancestors. "
>
> **– Wilbur Wright**

WHAT YOU NEED

- a pencil
- card stock
- scissors
- a paper clip
- tape
- a thin drinking straw
- an extra-wide straw
- pliers

- old felt-tip pen with a long plastic cap
- a bradawl (a tool for boring holes) or a large, sharp needle
- a long, thin elastic band
- a wooden skewer

1

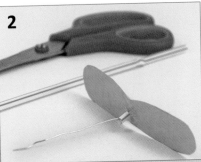
2

Step 1

Draw a **propeller** on the card stock and cut it out. Twist it gently to angle the propeller blades in different directions. Straighten out the paper clip. Push it through the middle of the propeller. Bend about 0.5 inches (1 cm) of the clip over at the end. Tape it against the propeller to hold it in place.

Step 2

Cut a 0.2-inch (0.5 cm) length of drinking straw. Thread it onto the paper clip.

3

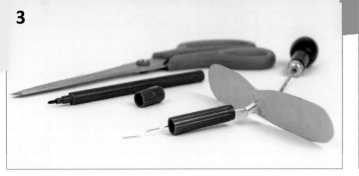

Step 3

Remove the felt-tip pen lid. Ask an adult to make a hole through the top of it, right in the middle. They can use the bradawl or needle. Push the paper clip through the hole from the top. It should be able to turn. If it doesn't, make the hole bigger.

4

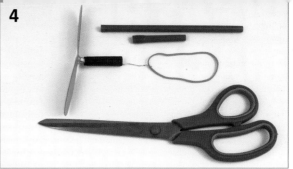

Step 4

With an adult to help, use the pliers to bend the straight end of the paper clip into a hook shape. Loop the elastic band into the hook. If the wider straw has a bendy part, cut that end off now.

5

Step 5

Use the wooden skewer to push the other end of the elastic band inside the straw and out at the other end. Cut about a 0.5-inch (1 cm) piece of the thin straw. Push it through the end of the elastic band to hold it in place.

6

Step 6

Now fit the pen lid over the end of the straw. If it doesn't fit over the straw, line up the lid and the straw. Then tape around them to hold them together.

7

Step 7

Cut a wing shape, a tail fin, and a tail wing from the thinner card stock. Tape them to the straw, while avoiding propeller. Trim them to fit if they are too big.

8

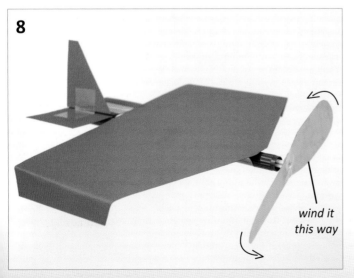

wind it this way

Step 8

To make the plane work, twist the propeller until the elastic band is tightly wound. Then let the plane go. It will only work if you twist the propeller in the right direction!

HOW PROPELLERS WORK

As a propeller turns, it slices through the air. Its angled blades push air backwards. This then pushes the propeller and the plane forward. Remember, a propeller also needs a source of power to turn it. In your model, the source of power is an elastic band. For the Wright brothers, it was a lightweight gasoline engine.

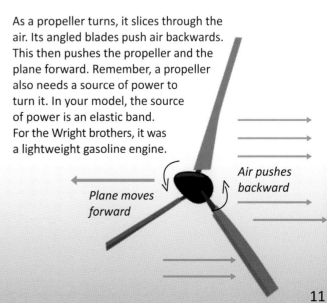

Plane moves forward

Air pushes backward

WEATHER MACHINE

Make a barometer to detect air pressure. **This can help you to forecast the weather.**

Lucien Vidie's barometer design

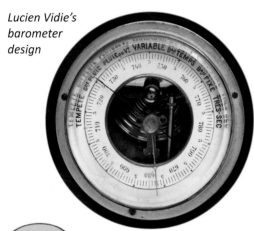

LUCIEN VIDIE

(1805–1866)

In 1843, French scientist Lucien Vidie developed a new type of **barometer**. Barometers measure air pressure. At that time, they existed for 200 years, but they were hard to move around. They used a container of liquid such as water or **mercury**. In Vidie's version, he used a sealed metal box called an **aneroid cell**. Air pressure changes affected the shape of the box and a set of levers recorded the results on a dial.

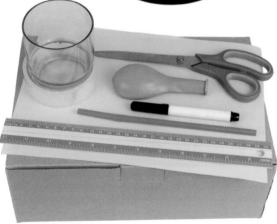

WHAT YOU NEED

- a glass jam jar or tumbler
- a balloon
- scissors
- tape
- a drinking straw
- a shoebox or other similar box
- a ruler
- plain paper
- a pen

Step 1

Cut the end off the balloon using the scissors. Stretch the rest of the balloon over the top of the jar. Make it as flat as possible. Use tape to hold it in place around the sides.

Step 2

Cut off the tip of the straw at a sharp angle to make a pointer. If the straw is bendy, use the straight end to make the pointer.

3

Step 3

Press the other end of the straw flat. Use a small piece of tape to attach it to the middle of the balloon skin.

4

Step 4

Cut a piece of paper that will fit onto the side of the box. Working up from the bottom of the paper, use the ruler and pen to mark a dot every 0.2 inches (0.5 cm).

5

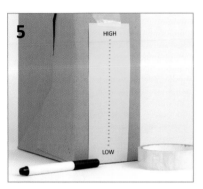

Step 5

Draw a line at the level of each dot to make a scale. Write "high" at the top of the scale and "low" at the bottom. Tape the paper onto the box.

6

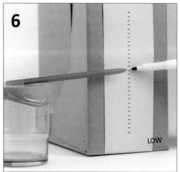

Step 6

Stand the glass next to the box, so that the straw points to the scale. Mark a dot to show the level of the straw.

7

Step 7

Leave the barometer in a place where it won't change temperature. (Changing temperatures affect the reading.) Check it at the same time each day to see if it shows higher or lower pressure.

> Low pressure is more likely to cause rain and wind. High pressure usually means calmer, sunnier weather.

AIR UP, AIR DOWN

The weight of the air around Earth causes air pressure. This changes in each place as air moves around. When air pressure is high, air piles up and sinks, pressing down on the balloon skin. When air pressure is low, the balloon skin rises again. In this invention, the straw acts as a lever. When the balloon skin moves up or down, the straw moves the opposite way.

WHAT'S IT GOT TO DO WITH THE WEATHER?

When air pressure is low, surrounding air rushes and swirls in. This movement causes wind. Air then gets pushed upward and gets cooler, leading to clouds and rain. High pressure makes air sink and spread out, so it's calmer and less cloudy.

BUBBLES GALORE

Build your own bubble machine and fill the air with bubbles!

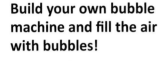

LAWRENCE WELK (AND HIS BAND)

(1903–1992)

Lawrence Welk wasn't actually an inventor. He was an American band leader, accordionist, and TV host in the 1950s and 1960s. He's remembered for using machines to fill the stage with bubbles as he performed. To this day, no one knows who actually made the machines. Some say Welk and his band first found a bubble-making machine in a hotel in the 1930s. Then they began making and using their own. "Lawrence Welk" bubble machines were later made and sold as toys.

WHAT YOU NEED

- Eight or more small bottles of bubbles with plastic blowers
- an old, unwanted CD
- a wide plastic tub, such as an ice cream tub
- a wooden spoon with a straight handle
- extra large wire paper clips or stiff garden wire with wire cutters
- duct tape or other strong tape
- scissors
- a battery-powered mini fan
- extra bubble mixture

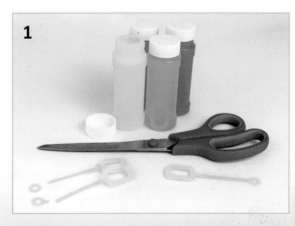

1

Step 1

Take all the blowers out of the bubble bottles. Rinse them clean and dry them well. Use scissors to snip off their handles, leaving the stems on.

2

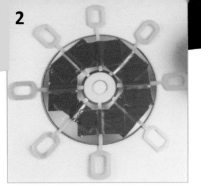

Step 2

Use strong tape to attach the bubble blowers to the printed side of the CD. They should stick out all around the edge.

3

Step 3

Fit the spoon handle into the hole in the CD. It will probably be loose. Wrap duct tape around the middle of the handle until it makes a tight fit.

4

Step 4

Straighten out a paper clip. Ask an adult to cut a length of garden wire about 8 inches (20 cm) long. Wind the middle section of the wire around the end of the spoon handle so it fits loosely.

5

Step 5

Tape the ends of the wire to the outside of the tub. Do the same with another paper clip or wire at the other end of the spoon handle. Tape it to the other side.

6

Step 6

Check that the CD can spin freely in the tub, without any of the bubble blowers hitting the bottom or sides. If they do, move the wires higher up, or switch to a larger tub.

7

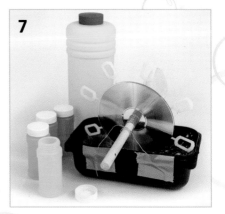

Step 7

Pour the bubble mixture from your bottles into the tub. Top up with extra mixture until it covers the lowest bubble blower.

8

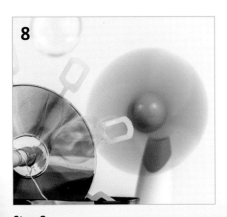

Step 8

Stand the fan next to the tub, pointing at the blowers. If your fan is too small for this, tape it to the side of the tub instead. Switch the fan on, and turn the spoon handle.

WORKING TOGETHER

We call this a **compound machine**, which is a machine that's made up of two or more basic machines working together. This machine makes use of a turning wheel so the bubble blowers dip in and out of the mixture. It also uses a propeller. A fan is a simple propeller that pushes air forward to make a breeze.

AT THE TOUCH OF A TOE

You've probably used a pedal trash can, but have you thought about how they work? Find out and make your own.

LILLIAN GILBRETH

(1878–1972)

American engineer Dr. Lillian Gilbreth was an expert in saving time and energy. She studied **psychology** and **engineering**. Dr. Gilbreth invented products that made everyday tasks easier. For example, she disliked doing chores. She came up with ideas to make them less stressful. Door shelves in a fridge, the electric can opener, and the pedal trash can were some of her inventions. We still use these inventions today.

WHAT YOU NEED

- a medium-sized cardboard box
- packing tape
- a ruler
- a marker or pen
- a craft knife or scissors
- a large wooden spoon
- card stock
- craft glue
- duct tape
- two wooden rulers or flat spatulas
- patterned paper to decorate

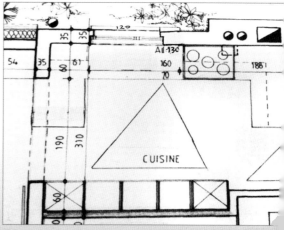

Gilbreth invented the "work triangle" model of kitchen design. This is still used today.

Step 1

Tape the cardboard box shut with the packing tape. Mark a line around three sides of the box, about 0.5 inches (1 cm) below the top. On the final side, draw a dotted line.

Step 2

With an adult to help, use scissors or a craft knife to cut along the three solid lines. Score the dotted line by lightly running the knife or scissors along it.

Step 3

Fold upward along the dotted line to make a flapping lid. Tape down any loose flaps inside the base or lid.

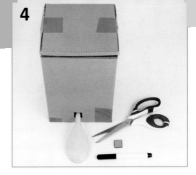

Step 4

Cut a hole just under 1 inch by 1 inch (2.5 cm by 2.5 cm) in the front of the box, about 1 inch (2.5 cm) above the base. Push the spoon handle into the hole. When you press on the spoon "pedal," the handle end inside should lift up.

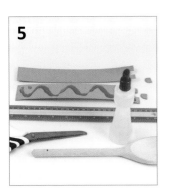

Step 5

Cut two strips of card stock, 1 to 1.5 inches (2.5 to 4 cm) wide and slightly longer than the height of the box. Cut a notch in the bottom of each strip, the same width as the spoon handle. Glue the two strips together.

Step 6

Push the double strip down to fit over the end of the spoon handle, inside the box. Trim the top of the strip so that it just touches the inside of the box lid when it's closed.

Step 7

Use duct tape to attach the top of the strip to the underside of the lid, about 1 to 1.5 inches (2.5 to 4 cm) away from the hinge.

Step 8

Tape the two rulers underneath the box, one on each side, so they stick out as far as the spoon pedal. These stop the can from tipping forward. Turn the can upright and test it.

LILLIAN'S LEVERS

The pedal in a pedal can is a simple lever. When you push one end down, the other end pushes up to lift the lid. The lid itself is a lever, too. The upwards movement close to the hinge makes the front of the lid lift up much farther.

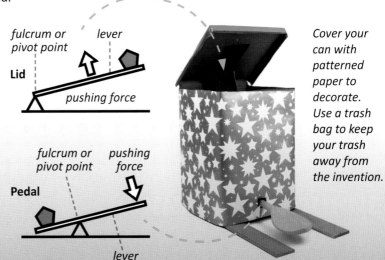

fulcrum or pivot point   lever

Lid

pushing force

fulcrum or pivot point   pushing force

Pedal

lever

Cover your can with patterned paper to decorate. Use a trash bag to keep your trash away from the invention.

SNACK MACHINE

Make your own vending machine based on a 2,000-year-old design.

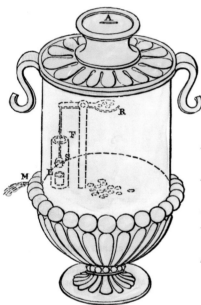

A drawing of Hero of Alexandria's vending machine, showing the working parts inside.

HERO OF ALEXANDRIA

(10–70 C.E.)

Hero of Alexandria was Greek, but lived in Egypt. He was an engineer and inventor who came up with all kinds of machines. Despite living 2,000 years ago, many of his ideas were modern. For example, he thought of a robot on wheels and automatic doors. He also thought of a **mechanical** puppet theater and the world's first vending machine. Temples even used Hero's vending machine to share holy water. We think our cardboard version that gives out candy is a bit less messy!

WHAT YOU NEED

- two small, sturdy cardboard packaging boxes
- a larger box with a lid, such as a large shoebox
- tape
- strong packing tape
- scissors
- extra-large wire paper clip, or garden wire with wire cutters
- a drinking straw
- a craft stick or small ruler
- a paper cup
- a small elastic band
- card stock
- coins
- small candies

18

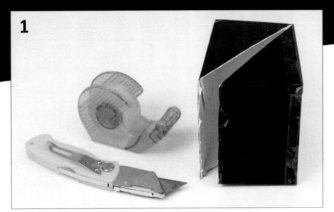

Step 1

Tape one of the small boxes shut. With the help of an adult, cut across each end from one corner to the other. Cut along one edge between the diagonal cuts, so that the box can flap open. This is the dispensing box.

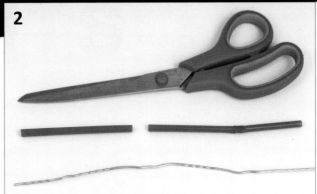

Step 2

Straighten out the paper clip or cut a length of garden wire about 8 inches (20 cm) long. Cut a length of drinking straw slightly shorter than the width of the small box. Thread it onto the wire.

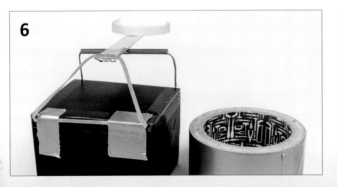

Step 3

Bend the two ends of the wire down, leaving a straight bridge in the middle. Tape the ends of the wire to the back of the box. This should be behind the hinge, so that the straight part sticks up above the box.

Step 4

Cut the base off the paper cup to make a small round tray. Cut off one side to leave a flat edge that is just over 1 inch (2.5 cm) long. Tape the tray to the end of the stick or ruler. Make sure the flat edge of the tray faces away from the stick.

Step 5

Now use tape to attach the middle of the stick or ruler to the top of the straw. Make sure the tray faces away from the box. It should be able to tip up and down like a seesaw.

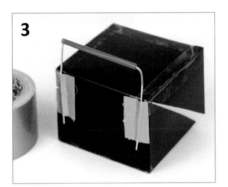

Step 6

Above the box, loop the elastic band over the other end of the stick or ruler. Use strong tape to attach the elastic band to the box in two places, as shown in the photo. When you press down on the tray, the box flap should open a little bit.

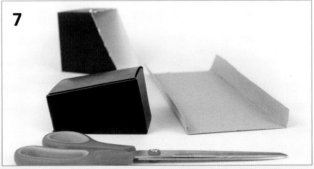

Step 7

Cut a piece of card stock about 4 inches (10 cm) wide and 8 inches (20 cm) long. Fold the sides up about 0.5 inches (1 cm) to make a slide. Take the second small box. Cut it off at an angle, making a sloping base for the card stock slide to rest on.

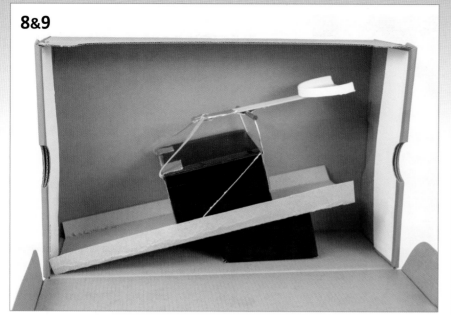

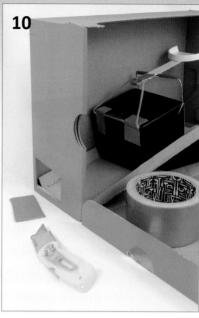

Step 8

Stand the larger box on its side. Stand the slide on its base inside. The bottom of the slide should touch the end of the box. Take the dispensing box you made and rest this at the top of the slide. It should face downwards.

Step 9

Check that everything fits inside the larger box. Also check that the stick can still move up and down, making the box lid open and shut. If not, make the slide shorter or the slide base lower. You could also switch to a bigger box if it still doesn't work.

Step 10

Once you're happy with it, tape the base to the bottom of the outer box. Place the dispensing box on the slide. Cut a hole in the outer box at the bottom of the slide for the candies to come out.

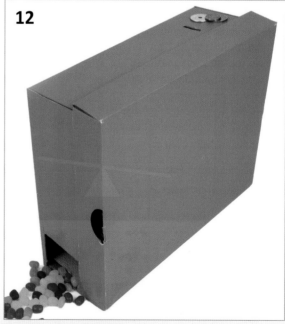

Step 11

Cut a coin slot in the top of the outer box, right above the tray on the end of the stick. Take the dispensing box out and put some candies inside. Close it and put it back in position. Tape it in place.

Step 12

Drop a large coin through the slot. It should hit the tray and lift the front of the box open for a moment, until the coin slides off and the box closes again. This will release a small handful of candies. If it works, put the outer lid on to hide the mechanism.

LIFTING LEVER

Although this vending machine is for candies instead of water, it works exactly the same way as Hero's did. When you drop a coin in, it pushes down a lever and the other end lifts up. The lever then pulls up the lid to let some of the candies out until the coin falls off and drops back down. In Hero's version, the lever lifted a plug at the bottom of a container of water. It let a little water out until the plug came down again.

A MACHINE FOR EVERYTHING

Hero's idea is still popular! There are now millions of vending machines all over the world. You can get all kinds of things from vending machines. Some have live crabs and lobsters, hot pizza, books, fresh lettuce, make-up, and even socks!

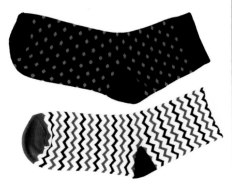

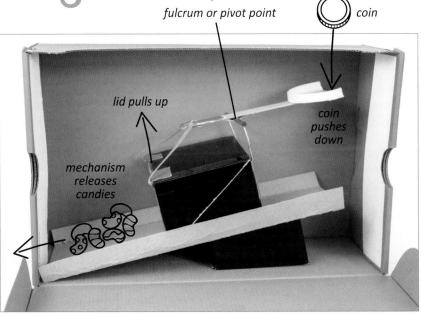

fulcrum or pivot point   *coin*

lid pulls up

coin pushes down

mechanism releases candies

A food and drinks vending machine

FLAPPING BIRD

Build your own bird automaton that bobs up and down and flaps its wings.

Fi Henshall's automaton Secretary Bird.

> The range of things that can be achieved merely by the turning of a handle intrigues me.
> — **Fi Henshall**

FI HENSHALL

(1981–)

Automatons are machines that make mechanical movements. These are often in the form of model people or animals. They date back to ancient times and are a popular form of art. British sculptor Fi Henshall is an artist who makes automatons. She uses wood, wire, and old tin boxes. Her art often features flying animals, women, mythical creatures, and small machines. By turning a handle, the models move. Sometimes, they even make sounds.

WHAT YOU NEED

- craft foam or thick corrugated cardboard
- scissors
- a marker
- strong glue or a hot glue gun
- a bradawl (a tool for boring holes) or thick needle
- wooden skewers
- tape
- a hole punch
- a cork
- strong card stock
- four small metal paperclips
- wire cutters
- a pipe cleaner
- three bendy drinking straws
- a small, sturdy cardboard box with a separate lid
- colorful tissue paper or wrapping paper

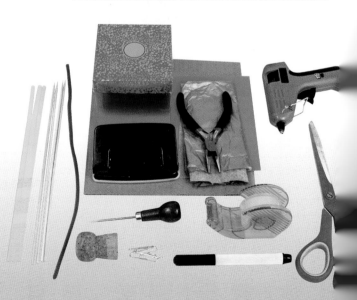

1

2

Step 1

On your craft foam or cardboard, draw six circles. They should each be about 1 inch (2.5 cm) across. Draw around a circular object to make sure they are all the same. Cut the circles out and glue three of them together in a neat stack.

Step 2

Mark a dot on the top of the stack between the center and the edge. With the help of an adult, use the bradawl or thick needle to make a hole through all three circles where the dot is. Put glue into the hole.

3

4

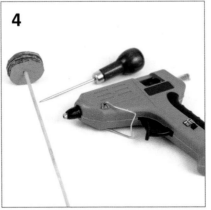

5

Step 3

Make two holes on opposites sides of your box, about halfway down. Stick the wooden skewer into one side, through the hole in the circles, and out of the other side. Make sure the circles are about halfway along the skewer. When you turn the skewer, the circles should bob up and down.

Step 4

With the help of an adult, glue two of the remaining circles together. Make a hole through the center. Stick the blunt end of a wooden skewer into the hole.

Step 5

Make a hole in the middle of the lid of the box. Use the scissors to make it wider. Cut a piece of drinking straw about 1 inch (2.5 cm) long and fit it into the hole. Wrap the straw in a layer of tape to make it a tight fit.

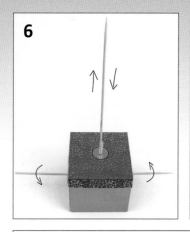

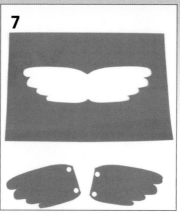

Step 6

Thread the skewer you made in Step 4 up through the straw. The end with the circles should be underneath the lid. Place the lid onto the box. When you turn the horizontal skewer, the vertical one should move up and down. This is because the circles turn against each other.

Step 7

Now make your bird. Draw two long, feathered wing shapes on the card stock. Cut them out. Use the hole punch to cut two holes in the wider end of each wing.

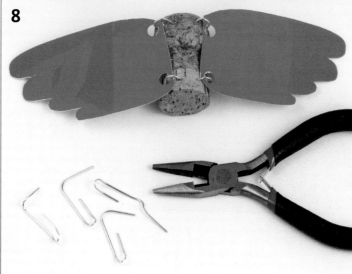

Step 8

Ask an adult to cut a loop off each paper clip with the wire cutters to make four small U-shapes. Loop these through the holes in the wings. Push the ends into the sides of the cork. Check that the wings can move up and down.

Step 9

Use the bradawl to make a hole in one end of the cork near the top. Cut a piece of pipe cleaner about 1.5 inches (4 cm) long. Stick one end into the hole. Make a head from a triangle of card stock folded in half. Glue it onto the pipe cleaner and draw on eyes.

Step 10

Cut feather shapes from the tissue or wrapping paper. Glue them to the bird's head and tail. Make a hole in the underside of the cork using the bradawl. Gently push the vertical skewer into it.

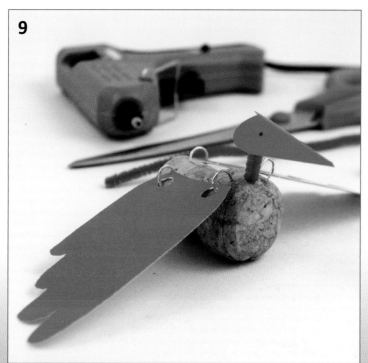

11

Step 11

Cut off the long ends of two drinking straws to make two short bendy sections. Bend them at right angles. Tape them to the undersides of the bird's wings, with one part of each straw pointing down.

Step 12

Make two holes in the top of the box next to the sides. Push two more skewers down into the holes. Be careful to avoid the horizontal skewer inside. Cut the tops of the skewers off to level with the wings.

Step 13

Fit the two skewers into the straws under the bird's body. Make sure they hold the wings steady, but can still move. Turn the horizontal skewer. The bird should move up and down. It should also flap its wings.

12

13

TWEAK IT

You may need to adjust the parts to make everything work well. Make sure the two circles inside the box are still lined up. If the wings don't move well, adjust the positions of the straws.

CHANGING MOVEMENTS

The flapping bird machine changes one type of movement into another. This is an important part of technology. Many machines, such as car engines, use this kind of movement to work.

The horizontal skewer is a **crankshaft**. This means it moves in a circle **motion**. The shape of the circles attached changes the motion into an up and down or side-to-side movement. Engineers call this **reciprocating motion**.

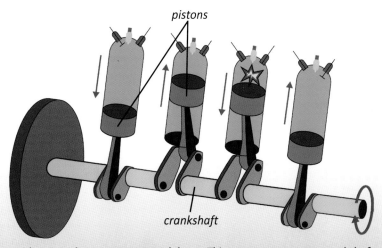

*Inside a car, **pistons** move up and down. This movement turns a crankshaft, which makes the wheels spin around. An up-and-down movement turns into a rotating movement. This is the opposite of how the bird works.*

JITTER CRITTER

Make your very own vibrating, jumping robots.

I want to create objects that are both humorous, and unpredictable in behaviour.
— Chico Bicalho

WHAT YOU NEED

- a vibrating toothbrush or a mini vibration motor from an electronics store
- a coin battery, such as a watch battery
- pliers
- scissors
- tape
- a plastic bottle top
- a large needle or bradawl (a tool for boring holes)
- colored paper clips

CHICO BICALHO

(1960–)

Chico Bicalho is a Brazilian artist, designer, and photographer. He created mini-robots called Critters. These became a popular toy around the world.

Critters use clockwork motion to work. The clockwork motion creates vibrations. This is how they jump, dance, and move around on their wire legs. Clockwork is not the only way to make robots. Vibration works, too. This is called a vibrobot.

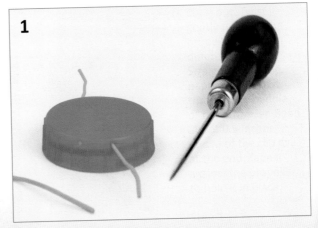

1

Step 1

Ask an adult to make six holes in opposite sides of the bottle top. They can use a large needle or bradawl. Straighten out three paper clips. Push them through the holes to make the insect legs.

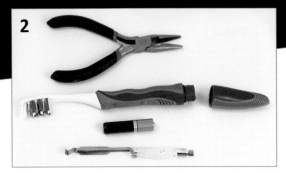

Step 2

If you are using a toothbrush, ask an adult to take it apart to get the motor out. The motor will be near the battery. An adult can remove it using pliers.

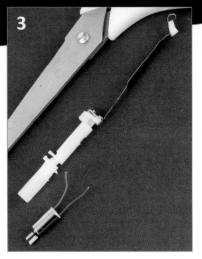

Step 3

With an adult, cut the two wires attached to the motor. Leave the wires as long as possible. Pull out the motor. Ask an adult to use scissors to remove some plastic coating from the ends of the wires.

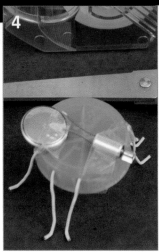

Step 4

Use a small, narrow piece of tape. Attach the motor to your bottle top on one side. Use another piece of tape to stick the end of the red wire underneath the coin battery.

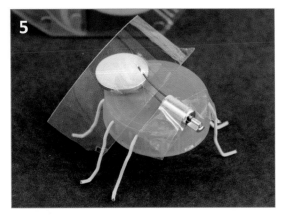

Step 5

Take another piece of tape and stick it to the end of the blue wire. Press it onto the top of the battery. Stick the tape down onto the toy insect to hold the wires and battery in place.

MAKING IT SHAKE

A motor makes a spinning motion when electricity runs through it. For a vibration motor, there is an "offset" weight attached to it. This is a weight that is heavier on one side. When it spins, this shakes the motor and the object to which it's attached.

Vibration motors are part of everyday life. We use them in toothbrushes, toys, and cell phones (to make them buzz).

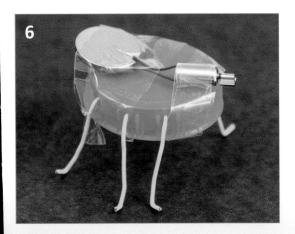

Step 6

When you press down the blue wire, it should connect the battery to the motor and make it start spinning. Put your invention on a flat surface. Let it go!

MORE BOTS

Try attaching your vibration motor to:

- A toothbrush head (ask an adult to cut it off for you)
- A pizza saver or box stand (three-legged plastic stand from a delivery pizza box)

ROBOT TENTACLE

Need to grab something, or tap your friend on the shoulder? Use your tentacle!

"What futures do we need?...
What worlds do we want to create?
– Kaylene Kau"

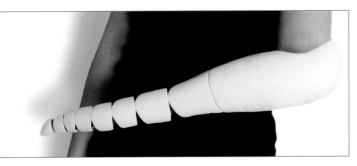

*Kaylene Kau's **prototype prosthetic** tentacle arm replaces the lower half of the human arm. It can grab objects by curling up like an octopus tentacle.*

WHAT YOU NEED

- foam pipe insulation tubing (from a hardware store)
- duct tape or other strong tape
- a marker
- a pencil
- a ruler
- scissors
- drinking straws
- strong string
- a metal keyring

KAYLENE KAU

(1988–)

In 2010, a Taiwanese-American student named Kaylene Kau made newspapers around the world. She designed an artificial arm. This arm worked like an octopus arm. (An octopus arm is also called a tentacle.) To make this arm, Kaylene did something a little different. She did not copy the full set of movements of a human arm. Instead, she studied what people who use artificial arms do. From this, she made the tentacle to hold objects. That way, people could hold objects with the tentacle while using their other working arm.

Step 1

Cut a length of tubing about 20 inches (50 cm) long. Mark a long V-shape along it. Start from a point on one end and widen to opposite sides of the tube at the other.

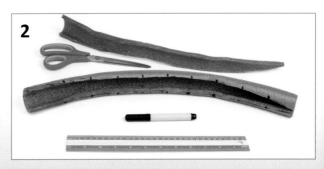

Step 2

With an adult to help, cut out the V-shape. Leave a piece of tube that is more tube-shaped at one end and narrower toward the other. Mark a dot every 2 inches (5 cm) along it.

3

4

5

Step 3
At each dot, cut a smaller V-shape out of the side of the tubing. These should be just under 1 inch (2.5 cm) wide and just under 1 inch (2.5 cm) deep. Do the same along the other side so that the V-shapes line up.

Step 4
The tube can now curl up in sections. Count how many sections you have. Cut the same number of short lengths of drinking straw, each just under 1 inch (2.5 cm) long.

Step 5
Starting at the wider end, push the two sides of the first section together. Cut a small piece of tape. Press it onto the inside of the tube to keep the two sides in place.

6

7

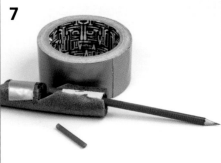

8

Step 6
Put a piece of straw between the two edges. Stick another piece of tape over the top. This will hold the section together with the straw inside the join.

Step 7
Do the same for all the other sections. For the smallest sections, use the end of a pencil to press the tape against the join from the inside.

Step 8
Thread a long piece of string through all the straws. At the smallest section, tie it tight and secure it with a piece of tape. Tie the other end of the string to the keyring.

> To use the tentacle, hold it by the base and pull the keyring to make it curl up.

TUBE CONTROL

When a tube curls over to one side, it gets shorter on that side. You can control a tube or cylinder shape by shortening strings along the side (or sides) to make it curl up. This is how our fingers work. They use string-like tendons inside our hands. Octopus tentacles and elephant trunks work this way, too.

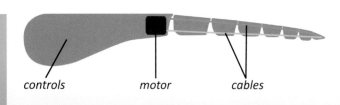

controls   motor   cables

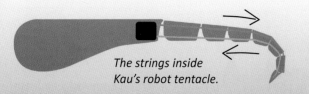

The strings inside Kau's robot tentacle.

GLOSSARY

air pressure The pushing force created by the weight of the air in the atmosphere

aneroid cell A sealed container with a vacuum inside, which is a space that has nothing in it, not even air. This can make a barometer without using liquid.

Archimedes screw A pump invented by Archimedes. This uses a turning screw to move water from a lower to a higher level.

automaton A mechanical model that can be made to move, usually by turning a handle

barometer A device for measuring air pressure

cable A thick rope or cord used in construction or transportion

compound machine A machine made up of two or more simple machines

crankshaft A long rod or circular object that can rotate, found in some types of machines

energy The power to do work or make things happen

engineer Someone who designs or builds machines, structures, or engines

engineering The theory and design of machines, engines, and structures

fulcrum The point that a lever pivots or rotates around

gears Wheels that lock into each other and make each other turn. They do this as a way of changing the speed of rotating, spinning, or turning motion.

glider An aircraft that flies without an engine, using gravity or air currents

lever A simple machine made up of a solid bar that turns or pivots around a point

mechanical Something that works using a machine or machines

mercury A silver metal. This is liquid at room temperature.

motion Another word for movement. It is often used by scientists and engineers.

pistons Cylinders or discs that move back and forth inside a tube. They are inside some types of machines.

propeller A device made of two or more angled blades. It rotates to push against a fluid, such as water or air.

prosthetic An artificial or replacement body part

prototype An early working model or first version of an invention

psychology The study of the human mind and personality

pulleys Wheels with cords or cables that move around them, used to pull or lift an object

reciprocating motion A repeating up-and-down or side-to-side movement

satellite A device put into orbit around a planet, moon, or other object in space

simple machines Machines that do one simple job

WEBSITES

**Exploratorium Science Snacks:
Engineering and Technology**
www.exploratorium.edu/snacks/
subject/engineering-and-technology

NeoK12 Simple Machines
www.neok12.com/Simple-Machines.htm

Animated Engines
www.animatedengines.com

Science Trek: Simple Machines
http://idahoptv.org/sciencetrek/topics/
simple_machines/facts.cfm

WEBSITES ABOUT MAKING

Tate Kids: Make
www.tate.org.uk/kids/make

PBS Design Squad Global
http://pbskids.org/designsquad

Instructables
www.instructables.com

Teachers Try Science: Kids Experiments
www.teacherstryscience.org/kids-experiments

WHERE TO BUY MATERIALS

Staples
www.staples.com

The Home Depot
Tubing, wood, glue, and other hardware supplies
www.homedepot.com

Home Science Tools
www.homesciencetools.com

BOOKS

Jefferis, David. *Micro Machines*. Crabtree, 2006.

Law, Felicia and Gerry Bailey. *Stone Age Science: Simple Machines*. Crabtree, 2016.

Snedden, Robert. *Mechanical Engineering and the Simple Machines*. Crabtree, 2013.

Solvay, Andrew. *Civil Engineering and the Science of Structures*. Crabtree, 2013.

PLACES TO VISIT

The Tech Museum of Innovation
www.thetech.org

Exploratorium
www.exploratorium.edu

INDEX